World War II Spy

Written by Adrian Bradbury
Illustrated by Lee Sullivan

Contents

Spies

When countries go to war against each other, spies play an important role. A key element of war is knowing your enemy's strengths and weaknesses. The more information you have, the better you can plan. The spy's task is to gather this information without the enemy knowing and pass it back to his or her commanders.

Any information might turn out to be useful. How many people does the enemy have? What battle plans do they have? Who are their leaders? How can we get to them? And of course: how are *they* spying on *us*?

Some spies operate in their own country. They betray their homeland for a variety of reasons: money, fame or **dissatisfaction** with their government, for instance. Others might be blackmailed by an enemy into spying on their own country, and forced into revealing its secrets.

Some spies are sent into enemy countries to find out what's happening and report back. They might build up a network of contacts in that country to help them. Their life is full of danger. They live with the fear of exposure, day and night. These people are also known as secret agents.

Virginia Hall was one of the bravest and best.

Virginia Hall in 1941

Virginia Hall's early life

Virginia Hall was born on 6 April 1906 in Baltimore, on the east coast of the United States of America.

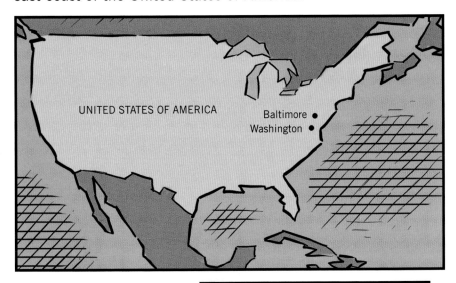

UNITED STATES OF AMERICA

Baltimore ●
Washington ●

Her father, Edwin Hall, was a successful businessman who owned a chain of cinemas. As well as their house in the city, the family owned Box Horn Farm, where Virginia spent much of her childhood.

Box Horn Farm

Virginia with her brother
at Box Horn Farm

Virginia and her family

Virginia's father took
his family on holidays
to Europe. This was
unusual in the early
20th century, when
travel was much more
expensive and many
American families didn't have much money and lived in
poverty. Virginia first visited Europe when she was only three
years old. Her regular trips allowed her not only to experience
different cultures and lifestyles, but also to begin to learn
different languages.

In the 1920s, when Virginia was ready to leave school, there were limited career opportunities for women. Although women in the USA had won the right to vote in 1920, many colleges were still male-only and there were few chances for a woman to get a good job. Single women could find work as nurses and teachers and as office or factory workers. Once married, women were expected to dedicate their lives to looking after their home and children. Virginia's plans were different. She hoped for a career overseas, so she needed to develop her ability in foreign languages.

Radcliffe College was one of the few women-only colleges. Virginia decided to continue her studies there, and moved to Cambridge, Massachusetts, 400 miles from her home.

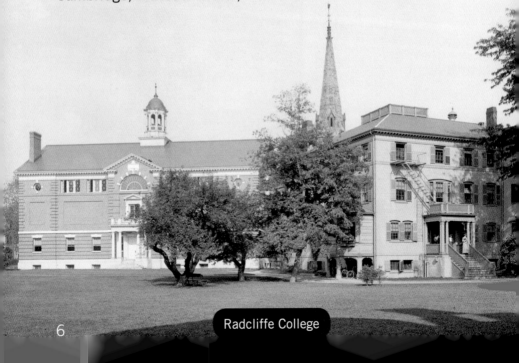

Radcliffe College

After just one year she moved to New York, where she studied languages at the all-female Barnard College. In 1926 Virginia crossed the Atlantic Ocean to continue her education at the Sorbonne University in Paris, France, before moving on, this time to Vienna in Austria. Here she graduated from the Konsular Akademie in 1929, before returning to the USA to complete her education at George Washington University in the capital city.

Diplomatic life

By the time Virginia was ready to look for work in the late 1920s, the USA was suffering an economic slump. This meant that money and employment were hard to find. She decided to seek a career abroad and in 1931 she was awarded a position as a **Consular Service** clerk at the US **Embassy** in Warsaw, Poland. This involved secretarial duties such as typing, taking phone calls, filing and arranging appointments. Confident, resourceful and fluent in French, German and Italian, Virginia was the ideal candidate. It took a good deal of courage for a lone female to venture into Eastern Europe, where life could be very dangerous in a land still unsettled following the upheavals of World War I.

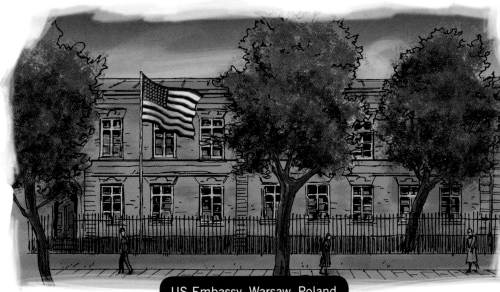

US Embassy, Warsaw, Poland

But Virginia was strong-minded and determined and was not deterred by the potential dangers. Although her typing and clerical skills were average, her dynamic personality was noted and admired by her superiors, and her career was progressing well.

After two years in Poland, Virginia requested a transfer and in April 1933 she took up a similar post in Smyrna, Turkey.

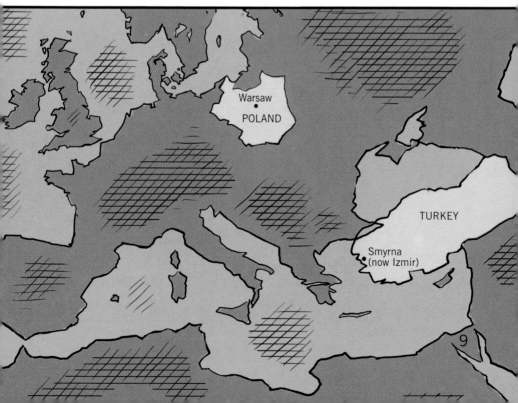

POLAND
Warsaw

TURKEY

Smyrna
(now Izmir)

In December 1933, Virginia rode out with friends on a hunting expedition into the countryside. Attempting to climb a fence while carrying her shotgun, her foot slid on the wet grass and the weapon slipped from her grasp. It went off, firing a mass of pellets into her foot. With no specialist medical aid at hand, her companions tore off strips from their clothing to bind the wound and stop the bleeding, then got her back to Smyrna as quickly as possible. But by the time a doctor was able to treat her wound, infection had already set in. **Antibiotics** had not been invented in those days, so any spread of infection could be fatal. There was no way to save Virginia's foot and a surgeon was forced to amputate her left leg just below the knee.

After a month of close monitoring, Virginia was transferred to the American hospital in Istanbul. Here she was assessed and declared fit for travel back to the United States. Once she was home and installed in the comfort of Box Horn Farm, Virginia was able to recover more quickly, from both the injury and the shock. Precise measurements were taken so that a wooden leg could be made for her. The wood was hollowed out to make the false limb lighter and a leather cover was fitted over the top. Leather straps laced up Virginia's thigh to keep the false leg in place and further elastic straps reached up to a belt around her waist. A woollen sock around the stump of her leg helped to prevent rubbing between her skin and the wood. The whole contraption weighed just over three kilogrammes.

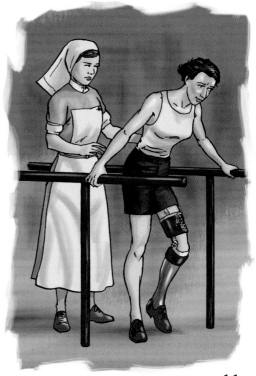

With typical good humour, Virginia nicknamed it "Cuthbert" and set to work learning how to walk again. Despite all the practice, she would walk with a limp for the rest of her life.

By the autumn of 1934 Virginia was fit enough to begin work again. Although Spain, Estonia and Peru were her three preferred locations, unfortunately there were no vacancies in those embassies, but Virginia was offered a post at the US **Consulate** in Venice, Italy. She accepted, beginning her new job in December.

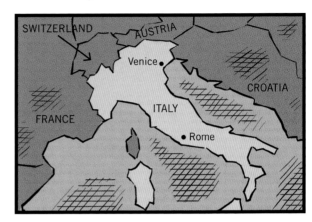

Virginia's plan had always been to become a Foreign Service officer. This would give her a lead role in running an embassy, representing the USA overseas. While in Venice she applied for promotion and started to take the necessary tests.

But before she was able to take the oral examination, bad news arrived. The **regulations** stated that amputation of any portion of a limb, except fingers and toes, made it impossible to qualify for entry into the Foreign Service. Numerous appeals were rejected, so Virginia decided to move on once again and in June 1938 she was transferred to the US Consulate in Tallinn, Estonia. She quickly realised that there was little chance of her progressing to the higher levels of responsibility, and in May 1939 she resigned.

Tallinn

THE SOVIET UNION (today called Russia)

ESTONIA

LATVIA

War

On 1 September 1939, under the command of the German Chancellor, Adolf Hitler, German troops invaded Poland. The country was occupied within 17 days and German troops then moved west, towards Belgium and France. Britain soon found itself drawn into a conflict against Germany. World War II had begun.

Adolf Hitler

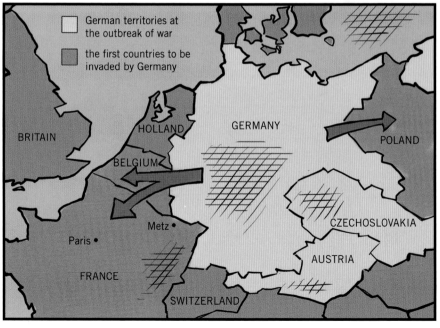

German territories at the outbreak of war

the first countries to be invaded by Germany

BRITAIN

HOLLAND

GERMANY

POLAND

BELGIUM

Metz •

Paris •

CZECHOSLOVAKIA

AUSTRIA

FRANCE

SWITZERLAND

At the outbreak of war, Virginia was living in Paris. As the German army advanced into France, she **enlisted** in the French ambulance service. After a few weeks of basic medical training she was posted to Metz, in the north-east of the country, where she endured long shifts as an ambulance driver. Virginia's job was to ferry wounded soldiers from the battlefield to temporary hospitals. Life was hard, with long hours of driving over bumpy fields and tough physical work helping soldiers into and out of the vehicle.

It was only when France surrendered in June 1940 and Hitler's army prepared to move into Paris, that Virginia knew she had to leave. Travelling by train across France, she crossed over the border into Spain, from where she was able to board a boat bound for England.

As soon as Virginia arrived in London she went to the US Embassy, where she was offered a job, again as a clerical assistant. Within weeks of her arrival in the capital, the German air force launched an all-out attack. Day and night their bombers flew over London, wreaking destruction and chaos in the streets below. Virginia was determined to return to France and rejoin the fight against what she saw as evil. At that time, however, the USA was not at war with Germany, so she volunteered her services to the newly formed British secret service, the Special Operations Executive (SOE).

Winston Churchill giving a speech

The SOE was formed in 1940 on the orders of the new British Prime Minister, Winston Churchill, "to set Europe ablaze" by waging an undercover war against the Germans who had occupied France. The organisation kept such a low profile that very few people in the country were aware that it existed. For the SOE Virginia was ideal spying material: female, non-British, an expert in languages and comfortable living in a foreign country. She would be able to move around and gather information without arousing the suspicions of the occupying Germans. The SOE willingly took her on and her training began.

All applicants, both men and women, had to undergo intensive training before they were sent out "into the field" on active duty. The first stage took place in remote mountain areas of Scotland and consisted of **gruelling** physical challenges as well as killing techniques. Trainees were taught how to kill silently using a short knife, an improvised weapon or their bare hands. Firearms training was also geared towards fighting the enemy up close, either with a handgun or a small machine gun.

Virginia was taught the essential skills of radio communication and using explosives – the destruction of buildings and trains would be one of her main objectives. Map reading and survival skills were also vital, as agents had to find their way to their target destinations after being dropped in by parachute.

Parachute training took place at Manchester Airport. The planes would have to fly low to avoid enemy radar, leaving the agent with no more than 15 seconds to open their canopy and make their landing. Each jumper had a small spade strapped to their leg so that they could bury their parachute after landing. But Virginia's wooden leg meant that a parachute drop was out of the question and she would need to travel to France by boat.

Virginia was taught how to pass unnoticed among the enemy by adopting and maintaining a convincing cover story. She closely studied local French customs and language, so that she could blend in naturally with the rest of the population and she learnt techniques of disguise to change her appearance. These often consisted of very small, but subtle, alterations, such as putting on a hat or glasses, parting her hair differently, or adopting a different style of walk – which was important in Virginia's case due to her wooden leg.

In the final stage of preparation, Virginia and her colleagues were given practical spying and **evasion** tasks. They had to show that they could think quickly, act decisively, maintain their cover and, if necessary, withstand interrogation or even torture.

When training was complete and the agents were ready to be flown out, they were issued with two sets of pills: the first was designed to keep them awake when they couldn't afford to sleep; the second was for use in case they were captured by the enemy – if they swallowed the deadly poison cyanide that it contained, they would die within 15 seconds. Many agents chose to die rather than give up other agents and their secrets.

As a US citizen, Virginia could enter France legally. For this reason, a cover story was created that would explain her presence in the country. She was to travel as a French-speaking American journalist sending back reports of the war in France to her superiors at the *New York Post*. As part of her cover, Virginia had applied for and been given a job at the newspaper, but they were not aware that she was also a spy.

article written by Virginia Hall for the New York Post, 4 September 1941

Bathroom Offices in Vichy

Reporter Finds Capital Crowded

By VIRGINIA HALL
Special Radio to The Post

VICHY, Sept. 4 —When you arrive in Vichy, it seems that the years have been rolled back. There are no taxis at the station waiting for the incoming guest, but half a dozen buses are waiting here for new arrivals to various destinations in town. A few one-horse shays are hopefully drawing about—mostly in vain. I took a bus—a "gazogene" which uses charcoal instead of gasoline —and was driven perilously through the narrow streets.

Vichy is a tiny town of hotels and lovely parks along the banks of the River Allier, built for the summer guests who used to come to take the cure. It is an infinitesimally small place to accommodate the government of France and the French Empire, but the hotels, large and small, have been requisitioned for government purposes and the impossible has been accomplished.

Vichy Votes Dakar Fund

Doriot Party Fights Petain

Lyons

In August 1941, a boat
carried Virginia to Lisbon
in Portugal, and from
there she took a train to
Vichy in France. Vichy
and the southern half of
France had not yet been
occupied by the German
army. This was a useful
place to be because when
France had surrendered
they had struck a deal

with Germany that a French government would remain in
place, based in Vichy. However, it was little more than
a "puppet" government, with Germany pulling the strings
from above.

Upon arriving in Vichy, Virginia registered with both the French
authorities and the American Consulate. She spent only two
weeks in the city, but this was long enough for her to send
home her first newspaper report, describing the food shortages,
rationing and **black market**. This, and later articles, were
important as they supported her cover as a newspaper reporter.

From Vichy, Virginia moved on to Lyons, where she was the contact for all agents that were parachuted into the area. She gave them information and supplied them with money. To this end, the SOE had provided Virginia with a huge supply of used French banknotes, which she carried strapped around her waist.

fake identification papers of other secret agents in the war

As an American journalist, Virginia was able to check into a hotel in Lyons, where she asked for a room that faced out on to the street. This allowed her to see what was happening outside, but it also had a second purpose: it was a place where she would be able to leave signals for any agents in the area. For example, a vase in the window might mean that she was in and available for a meeting. Removing the vase could indicate that she wasn't in. Putting yellow flowers in the vase might indicate danger, while red ones could say: "Important! Make contact immediately!" Meetings in person were always dangerous, as any suspicious behaviour might be noticed. Likewise, any messages passed on paper could be intercepted. Visual signals were a much safer option.

Virginia also needed to make contact with the local French Resistance. These were people who hated the German occupation and were willing to risk their lives to fight against it. Behind the normality of their regular day jobs, Resistance fighters would organise themselves into secret groups and do all they could to damage the German army's activities: disrupting transport, destroying vehicles and buildings, attacking and killing soldiers. Virginia was given the names of two French Resistance **sympathisers**. Due to their age or occupation these people might not have been in a position to actively fight the German army, but they were sympathetic to the cause and would help whenever they could.

Virginia soon contacted the names of the sympathisers she'd been given: Doctor Jean Rousset and Madame Germaine Guérin. They, in turn, introduced her to other trusted people.

It was important that Virginia knew without any doubt that her initial contacts were the right people, before revealing any secrets to them. They were therefore all given coded phrases. Virginia was to greet them in French with: "I come with news about Marie." Only when they gave the coded reply: "Would you like to speak to Marie Renard?" would she know that they were indeed the right people.

During the early years of the war, many French people were unwilling to **defy** the German army, fearful of the consequences if they were caught. Others thought that it was useless to fight against such a powerful enemy. As a result, active resistance was confined to small groups and individuals, working without any clear plan. German army vehicles might be **sabotaged**, goods stolen and soldiers ambushed or shot. Some resistance would be passive and therefore difficult for the German soldiers to prevent, for example workers might deliberately work as slowly as they possibly could. They weren't committing a crime, but they were making life difficult for the German army. Some braver people would produce home-printed leaflets or newspapers to give a different point of view from the biased information that would appear in the German-controlled official press and radio. Packaged in plain envelopes, these leaflets could be distributed to known sympathisers, who could then spread the word wider still.

It was Virginia's job to bring together lots of different people to produce an efficient, well-organised Resistance network.

home-printed newspapers

If a person was caught in possession of one of these leaflets they were punished. Beatings and torture were common, as the German authorities tried to get names of other Resistance members and many sympathisers were removed to prison camps. It wasn't just the German soldiers who needed to be treated with caution. Some French people were prepared to turn their fellow countrymen in for the chance of a reward. Soon after Virginia's arrival in Lyons, a notice appeared in a Vichy newspaper offering a reward of 10,000 francs to anyone who captured an enemy pilot or who gave the German army information that led to their capture. Women who assisted pilots who had crashed would be sent to a concentration camp in Germany, and men would be shot.

Because of this, Virginia had to be very careful. One careless word overheard by the wrong person could prove fatal, not just for her, but for her friends and contacts too. She would have been in no doubt about the consequences of capture – any person suspected of spying would face the severest punishments. This was illustrated by the example of Virginia's SOE colleague, Violette Szabo, codenamed "Louise". She was sent to central France to do a job similar to Virginia's, working with local Resistance groups. One night her car was stopped by two German soldiers. In the gun battle that followed her two French comrades were able to escape, but she was captured. Despite beatings and torture Violette refused to reveal any information. She was then taken to Ravensbrück prison camp in Germany, where she was later executed. Many other spies suffered a similar fate.

Violette with her husband, Etienne

With the help of her new friends, Virginia was able to set up a network codenamed "Heckler". **Allied** pilots would be told before their mission that if they crashed they should make their way to Lyons and try to make contact with the Resistance. They would then be able to contact Virginia and she would help them to get to Spain. Virginia would help them with a suitable cover story and get them false identity papers. Appropriate local clothing would be found and money provided. If the pilot was wounded, a sympathetic doctor would treat him in secret. Careful instructions would be given before the pilot was passed from one group of sympathisers to another, until he reached the Spanish border.

One of Virginia's trusted comrades, Robert Le Provost, had a
family shipping business in the southern port of Marseilles,
while another, Eugène Labourier, owned a fleet of trucks.
This was one useful escape route. The pilot could be taken
south in one of Labourier's trucks and, when in Marseilles, he
could travel by fishing boat, which would deliver him to a
Spanish port. The safest route, however, was a journey by truck
to Perpignan on the Spanish border, because it's easier to cross
a mountainous border without being spotted. There the pilot
would link up with a local Resistance guide who could lead
him, on foot, over the Pyrenees mountains and down the other
side into Spain.

Virginia's supplies of money were not limitless. She relied on regular deliveries from England and these generally arrived via SOE agents parachuted into the area. Before that could happen a suitable drop site needed to be found. This would be a large field away from prying eyes, with easy access and escape routes. Once the site was fixed, its coordinates would be radioed back to London and a time set for the drop. Planes would need to fly in low, without lights, navigating using rivers that reflected the light of the moon. When the "welcome committee" heard the drone of the engines they would signal with a flashlight. Once the plane had returned the signal, further lights would illuminate the drop zone.

As soon as the agent landed, his parachute would be buried and the group would make their escape before the German army could arrive. Sometimes the drop would be essential supplies rather than humans. Weapons, **ammunition**, explosives, wireless equipment, clothing and medical supplies would all be carefully packaged into tall metal canisters and the same drop procedure followed.

Despite the constant dangers, Virginia had succeeded in building up one of the most efficient Resistance networks in France. Without ever being truly safe, her American identity allowed her some degree of protection from suspicion, though this was soon to change.

On 7 December 1941, the Japanese air force launched a daring and destructive raid on the US naval base at Pearl Harbor, Hawaii. Within days, the USA and Britain had declared war on Japan and in return Germany had declared war on the USA. As an American, Virginia was no longer safe.

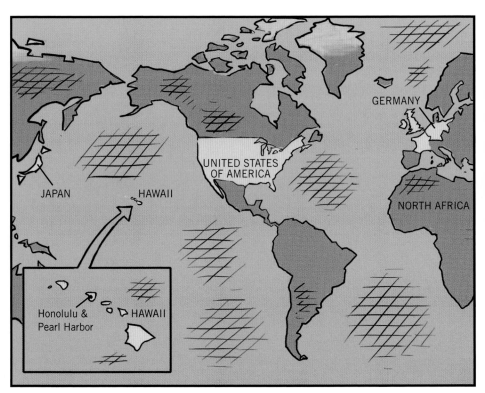

Britain and her allies had by now invaded north Africa and sent thousands more troops to fight there. Worried that the Allies might be planning to launch an invasion across the Mediterranean, Hitler ordered a huge number of troops into southern France. The whole area where Virginia was based was suddenly full of German soldiers, as well as Gestapo agents. The Gestapo was the feared German secret police force, who would not hesitate in dragging a person off the street for questioning, if they'd received information that the person had been acting illegally, though often this information was unreliable or untrue. Sometimes they might just be watching from their car and feel that someone was acting in some way suspiciously. Some innocent people who disappeared into the back of the black Gestapo cars never returned to their families.

It was becoming more and more difficult for Virginia to operate. Previously she had been able to meet contacts in cafés and bars, where it was quite natural for people to get together and chat. But now the German army was tightening its grip and everybody was considered a suspect. There were rumours that the Gestapo was on the trail of a foreign woman, possibly Canadian. Lyons was no longer safe for her.

Taking a train, Virginia arrived in Perpignan under the false name of Marie Monin. She met up with the local Resistance and negotiated a deal for a guide to take her and three other hunted men over the mountains to Spain. On the night of Thursday, 12 November 1942 they set off into the mountains from the small town of Lavelanet. Their arduous trek took them around 50 kilometres over rocky, snow-covered terrain, weighed down by backpacks. The freezing air made breathing difficult, especially near the top of the pass at 2,100 metres.

On their descent into Spain, they arrived at a tiny village where their guide led them to a **safe house**. From there, Virginia was able to send a coded message back to her SOE commanders in London, explaining her situation. She ended with the words: "Cuthbert is being tiresome, but I can cope." Unaware of her leg's nickname and assuming she was referring to an enemy, the reply came back: "If Cuthbert tiresome, have him eliminated."

The journey was not yet over, however. Virginia's plan was to reach the American Consulate in Barcelona, but before she could board a train she was detained by local police as her papers didn't contain the necessary entry stamp into Spain. After being held for several days, the US authorities intervened and Virginia was finally able to fly back to London. She had escaped just in time. The net had closed around her operation in Lyons, with many of her former comrades now in the hands of the Gestapo, betrayed by their countrymen. Virginia was now well-known to the the top generals who organised and controlled the German forces in France, so much so that "Wanted" posters could be spotted nailed to doors and posts. "La Dame Qui Boite" – "The Limping Woman" – was considered one of the Allied forces' most dangerous agents, the posters said. She must be found and destroyed.

a drawing of Virginia Hall produced by the Germans

Spain

After a few months of rest and recuperation, Virginia was posted to Spain. The SOE realised that the Gestapo now had a clear description of her, so sending her back to France would be too much of a risk.

Spain had so far refused to join the war on Hitler's side. They were still in the process of recovering from their own civil war and their leader, General Franco, didn't want to risk the threat of bombings or invasion by the British. Being so close to the main battleground of France, there were many agents in Spain. Virginia again posed as an American journalist, this time for the *Chicago Times*. She was told to settle herself in Madrid and work normally for a few months to establish her cover. She was then told to gather information and relay it back to London.

General Franco, head of state, Spain

This job was much less exciting than her active role in France, however, and within months Virginia had taken up the offer of a return to London. Here she worked with agents returning from France and helped to train those who where about to go out. Although she already had basic radio communication skills, Virginia took the opportunity to do a training course as a specialist radio operator.

a radio used during World War II

In November 1943, Virginia learnt that the British king, George VI, had chosen to bestow on her the award of MBE – Member of the British Empire. However, publicly receiving an award for spying would virtually ensure she would never be able to spy again, as she would become easily identifiable to the enemy. She realised that a visit to Buckingham Palace would blow her cover completely – there were many German spies operating in London – so she decided not to attend the ceremony.

King George VI

Back to France

Virginia was soon provided with an opening to return to France. Possibly inspired by the success of the SOE, the Americans had decided to set up their own secret service. Named the Office of Strategic Services (OSS), it was placed under the command of Major General "Wild Bill" Donovan. A highly **decorated** soldier and leader during the World War I, he was energetic, **charismatic** and fearless. Donovan had spent time in London and realised how important the input of the SOE was. As soon as Virginia became aware of the OSS set-up, she knew it could provide her with the chance to return to France. In March 1944 Virginia was given leave to approach the OSS and was immediately taken on. Soon she was posted back to France.

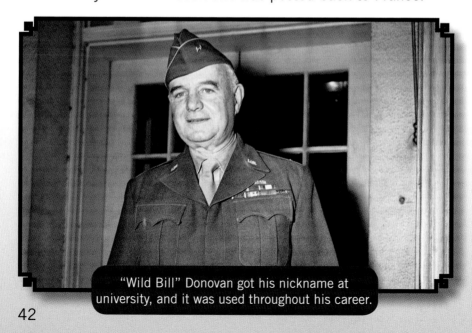

"Wild Bill" Donovan got his nickname at university, and it was used throughout his career.

In France, Resistance groups were now firmly established, but their activities carried with them even more terrible risks. If members of the Resistance were not captured or turned in, it was not unknown for 50 innocent people to be lined up against a wall and shot. This was an extreme punishment, but effective – Resistance members would be less willing to fight if they knew that innocent friends or family would be killed instead of themselves. And the Resistance now faced a new threat from their own people: the *Milice* was a group of French people who actively supported the German army. The *Milice* handed over members of the Resistance to the Gestapo for money. Because they operated in their home towns and villages, they were considered more dangerous than the German army, as they saw and heard everything that went on locally.

Virginia set off for France in March 1944. This time there was no thought of an American cover. She was to be an elderly French peasant, unrecognisable from the sophisticated journalist of her previous visit. Layers and layers of thick clothing filled out her figure, explaining the slow, shuffling walk that helped to disguise her limp. Her brown hair was dyed grey and pulled back into a bun, over which a headscarf was tied. She even underwent dental treatment to remove her fillings and replace them with typically French ones. No stone was left unturned. The German army was on the lookout for a tall, good-looking, intelligent, limping American journalist. They would hardly confuse her with the stooping, dirty, overweight peasant woman that would shortly arrive in their midst.

A whole pack of dog-eared cards and documents was supplied in the name of Marcelle Montagne: identity card, food ration card, clothing ration card, tobacco ration card, driver's licence, birth certificate, medical certificate, work permit and residence permit. If Virginia was caught without any of these, suspicions would be aroused. She committed to memory every fine detail of her new life story, as well as the maps that would direct her to her destination in rural France.

Unable to parachute, Virginia was taken across the Channel in a British Motor Gun Boat along with a male agent, Henry Laussucq, codenamed "Aramis", with whom she would be working. Their mission was in three parts: to set themselves up in a base within 100 kilometres of the south of Paris; to find three safe houses, one in Paris, one within easy reach of Paris and the other out in the countryside; finally, to set up in each of these houses two radio transmitters, one large and one small. Virginia was issued with half a million francs and given the codename "Diane".

Under cover of night, they used a rubber dinghy to paddle ashore on the rocky Brittany coast. One mile inland they made contact with a local Resistance member at his farm, before walking to the nearby town of Morlaix and boarding a train for Paris.

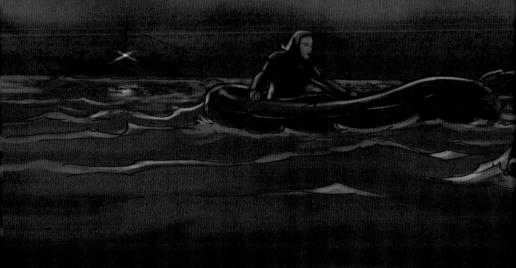

Again they contacted a Resistance
helper, and the next day they
made the journey out of Paris to
the village of Maidou. Virginia was
to base herself here, working for a
local farmer, Monsieur Lopinat.
Her days would be spent tending
his cows, cleaning his house and
cooking meals. She would live in
the tiny, one-roomed cottage he owned in the village.
It had neither electricity nor running water.

The cottage was isolated, however, which was an advantage for Virginia and upstairs was a dusty loft that was perfect for transmitting her radio messages. As she walked the cows around the quiet lanes and fields she was able to observe all around her. Virginia noted where German troops were stationed, as well as their numbers and movements. She located fields that might be suitable for parachute drops. All this she radioed back to England from the loft.

Virginia also devised another ingenious way of gathering information. Back home in America, at Box Horn Farm, she had learnt to make cheese. She knew that if she could do the same here, she would have an excuse for travelling into the local town of Crozant. There, Virginia would be able to eavesdrop on the German soldiers. They wouldn't realise that the scruffy, ignorant peasant woman selling them cheese was fluent in German and able to follow every word they said. The plan worked perfectly and her messages to London grew longer and more detailed.

Aramis, meanwhile, was a problem. Despite Virginia's warnings, he tended to talk too much, as well as insisting on coming from Paris to visit her at her cottage. Was he suspected? Had he been followed? And why would an old woman have a visitor anyway? One day he came with news that a new OSS agent sent to Paris had not made contact. Their immediate thought was that he may have been arrested. If so, had he told the Gestapo about her? Virginia made the decision to leave the village immediately. Through contacts in Paris, she was directed to the town of Cosne to meet the local chief of police, Colonel Vessereau.

Vessereau was not only a Resistance member himself, he also knew a whole host of local men, fiercely **patriotic** and anxious to take the underground war against Germany to a new level.

All they needed were the tools: money, weapons, explosives and leadership. Virginia could supply all of these. She had soon organised the men into four groups, each comprising 25 men. A parachute drop was arranged that supplied them with all the equipment they required.

two Royal Air Force groundsmen loading an airplane with supplies

members of the French Resistance retrieving supplies dropped by parachute

Virginia moved into the attic of a local farmhouse, an ideal base for sending her radio messages. She decided not to stay there too long as, to avoid difficult questions, it was best to keep moving. Sending messages from a radio transmitter, as Virginia regularly had to do, was a very dangerous business.

The German army used detector vans, which patrolled the streets and picked up signals coming from houses or offices. Whenever possible, agents would try to send messages from different locations to avoid detection, moving from one safe house to another between messages.

a mobile radio detector, which was used to pick up radio signals

If captured, a radio operator might be forced by his captors to send false messages back to England. For this reason a "bluff" was always used. This was a **prearranged** word or phrase that would indicate that the message was not being sent under the watching eyes of a German captor. The German army worked out this tactic, but for a long time they failed to realise that there was also a "double bluff" – a second phrase that confirmed that the message was reliable. If either was absent from a message, the listeners in London would know that their agent had been captured.

On 23 May 1944 Virginia received a message from London. They needed all the information she could provide as a matter of urgency. A "period of activity" was beginning.

Invasion

It had been common knowledge for some time that the British and American armies were planning to invade France.

At 9 p.m. on 1 June 1944, listeners to French radio heard the first line of a famous French poem read out in a personal message. The line, "The long sobs of the violins of autumn", was in fact a coded message that the Allied invasion would come some time soon. When the second line was read out on 5 June, this indicated that it would take place in the next 48 hours. Radio stations were frequently used to send coded messages that would mean nothing to anyone who hadn't been told the code.

It was Virginia's role both to gather information and to do all she could to upset German plans, so she and her teams set to work. Railway lines were blown up to slow down the movement of both German soldiers and supplies. Small groups of men would strap explosives to the rails during the night. The front wheels of the first morning train would crush small **detonators** laid across the rails and set off the explosives beneath, derailing the train and buckling the track. Holes were blown in main roads. Key bridges that the German army needed to move across were destroyed, while enemy explosives were removed from bridges that would be useful to the Allies. Telephone offices were blown up and vehicles sabotaged. Wherever they turned, the German army was attacked and **harassed**.

Although the Allied invasion took place on the Normandy beaches of north-west France, most of the German defences were still in the area around Calais, 320 kilometres away. This was mainly due to the work of another spy, the Spaniard Juan Pujol, codenamed "Garbo".

Working first from Portugal and then from England, he and his SOE handlers sent out false information to the German army.

Garbo invented whole networks of fake spies throughout the UK and simply radioed their "findings" to Germany. So trusted did he become that Hitler was fooled into believing Garbo's fictional evidence that the D-Day landings were merely a decoy and the main attack would then be launched around Calais.

Garbo in disguise

Normandy landings, 1944

Realising that her Resistance groups were now so well organised that they could operate without her, and that Brittany would soon be in Allied hands anyway, Virginia's OSS bosses ordered her south again. With nearly all trains being used to carry soldiers and vital supplies, she faced a long and tedious journey with hours of waiting. Eventually she found her way to the village of Le Chambon-sur-Lignon in central France. Here was an area that had seen little organised resistance, although there were many men keen to fight. It was Virginia's job to make sure they did.

Le Chambon

The villagers of Le Chambon had already shown themselves willing to defy the German army. Earlier in the war Hitler had begun to **discriminate** against the Jews, and French people were urged to join in by turning Jews over to the German authorities. Hitler was trying to convince the French that the Jews had caused all their troubles, so as to make the Jews the focus of their anger rather than the occupying German army. The people of Le Chambon refused to accept this, however. The town acted as a refuge for Jewish families and the residents would then help them to escape towards the Swiss border to the east. If German soldiers came into the village, the Jews would rush to hide in the forest. When the soldiers had gone, the locals would walk amongst the trees singing songs. This was the signal that it was safe to return.

At first, the proud local men were reluctant to take orders from a woman, let alone a foreign woman. They were Maquis – members of the French Resistance who hid in the wild, remote areas of France and formed themselves into units, fighting and then retreating into their hideouts. Virginia stood firm: if they wanted to receive the supplies she could provide, they would have to follow her commands. Virginia had a trusted second-in-command called Dédé and together they started to gather support. Soon she could count over 400 men ready and willing to take up the struggle.

a group of Maquis fighters

It was time to arrange the first parachute drop. The coded radio signal this time came through on 21 July 1944: "The daisies will bloom tonight. I say three times." This meant the delivery was due that night and there would be three planes. In all, 20 canisters were dropped, containing everything needed to equip a new Resistance group: machine guns, rifles, ammunition, explosives and detonators, knives and **bayonets**, clothes, boots, chocolate and money. There were even detailed instructions on how to use the explosives to carry out their acts of sabotage.

As more supplies were dropped and the Maquis became better drilled, the number of attacks on the German army increased. Almost every night a group would be sent out on a sabotage mission.

a member of the Maquis laying explosives

In her later report on her time in Le Chambon, Virginia noted some of the operations that took place between 27 July and 12 August 1944:

> Bridge blown at Montagnac, cutting road
>
> Four cuts on railroad Langogne–Brassac
>
> Freight train derailed in tunnel at Brassac
>
> Bridge blown on railway between Brioude – Le Puy
>
> Freight train derailed in tunnel at Monistrel and 15 metres of track blown up behind wrecking train and crew after it had gone into the tunnel to clear the wreckage
>
> Tunnel at Selignac made impassable by blowing up rails
>
> Railway track wrecked at Chamalières and locomotive driven into gulf below
>
> Telephone lines Brioude – Le Puy rendered useless – lines cut and wires rolled up and telephone posts cut down

a train derailed after the rails were blown up by the Resistance, 4 March 1944

Virginia didn't take an active part in any of these attacks. She was the organiser, giving the orders, and like many leaders she was too important to be risked. She spent her days cycling the high hills of the area, looking for suitable drop sites, talking to the men on the farms, gathering information from them and radioing it back to England each evening. One day she ventured into the local town of Le Puy to find a large number of German trucks and limousines. She discovered that the German High Command had moved their headquarters from Lyons and were taking up residence right there in Le Puy. This information was very important: as the Allies advanced they would naturally want to target the enemy commanders. Virginia wasted no time in relaying the news back to London.

There were approximately 1,500 men in Virginia's Maquis army and it was proving difficult to command. Each band had its own leader and disagreements were unavoidable. Virginia needed help. It arrived in late August in the form of three men: one British, one American and one French. This was one of many teams sent out by both the OSS and the SOE, designed to help organise the Resistance and Maquis all over France. As the German army's advance ground to a halt and their soldiers began to retreat, more French people were willing to actively fight against them. Having lived under their ruthless control for four years, they now wanted revenge as well as freedom. These new fighters, if properly organised, could provide the Allies with a deadly weapon, helping to destroy the German army.

men leaving their homes to join the Maquis

Some of this energy and fury was directed at French people who in the past had actively helped the enemy, indirectly resulting in the deaths of many brave men. When they realised that the German army was retreating, many of these **collaborators** claimed to have been members of the Resistance all along. But in many cases the locals would recognise them and remember what they had done during the German occupation. Maquis and true Resistance fighters would often execute collaborators rather than wait for them to be brought to trial. Female collaborators would have their heads shaved and were often spat at or stoned in the streets. Virginia was tireless in hunting down collaborators who had betrayed members of her own Resistance groups to the German army.

On 25 August 1944, the German officer in control of Paris surrendered the city to the Allies. Three days later the local German commander in Le Puy also surrendered. The German High Command had already left the town.

However, the war was not over yet. Some areas of France were still under German control, including the nearby city of St Etienne, and Virginia was still calling for supply drops. On 4 September she was informed that two men would be parachuted in that night. She went out to meet them, but was forced to find them in the darkness as the plane missed its target. One of the men was Lieutenant Paul Golliot from New York.

Realising that her skills could be put to better use elsewhere, Virginia set off with the two new arrivals. They made their way to Paris, where Golliot's family lived. During the previous few days he and Virginia had formed a close friendship, despite the unwritten rule that as an undercover agent it was dangerous to become too attached to anyone. Reporting to the military authorities in Paris, they received instructions that they were to fly back to London immediately because the OSS had more work for her to do.

Endgame

By December 1944 most of Western Europe was under the control of the Allied forces and the German army was in full retreat. The OSS expected the German leaders to make their way towards southern Germany and Austria, and were determined to track them down before they could escape altogether. They decided that the best way would be to activate the Resistance in the Alps and in Austria and that Virginia was the ideal person to do this – she had spent time in Vienna and also spoke fluent German. Virginia flew out to Italy together with Golliot, where they were to make their preparations to enter Austria. This time Virginia would be travelling as Anna Möller, a German citizen, codename "Camille". Golliot, codename "Henri", spoke no German and so would work entirely under cover with the Resistance.

The Maquis: armed and on the move, 1944.

However, on 10 April 1945, waiting on the Swiss border, their mission was postponed and they were told to await further instructions. They were soon redirected to Zürich, from where they would make their way over the mountains into Austria. It never happened. On 30 April, realising that final defeat was certain and not willing to be captured alive, Adolf Hitler committed suicide in Berlin. Virginia received a telegram to cancel her mission. Within days, the war was over.

soldiers in Paris, reading of Hitler's death in the paper

On 12 May, OSS chief Bill Donovan informed US President Truman that Virginia Hall had been awarded the Distinguished Service Cross (DSC), only to be given for "extreme gallantry and risk of life in actual combat with an armed enemy force". As she was the only American woman to receive the award in World War II, Bill Donovan suggested that the President might like to present the award himself.

Virginia had always made light of her achievements. On her final report she was asked to answer the question: "Were you decorated in the field?", to which she wrote: "No, nor any reason to be." It was her intention to continue with her work under cover and she was not willing to risk the future she had planned. The response from her Paris headquarters stated that she "... feels very strongly that she should not receive any publicity or any announcement as to her reward. She states that she is still operational and most anxious to get busy."

In the end the ceremony was delayed until Virginia was back in Washington. Bill Donovan presented Virginia with the DSC, with her mother as the sole witness.

Virginia receiving the DSC from Bill Donovan

After the war Virginia and Paul Golliot returned to America. Virginia looked for work in the Foreign Service and was again told that there were no openings. The OSS had been closed down, but a new agency had sprung up in its place: the Central Intelligence Group (CIG). Virginia signed on and spent the next year travelling through Europe, posing as a journalist, but once again working as a spy. She gathered information on political, economic and financial affairs, reporting back to her superiors in Washington. The CIG was soon closed and renamed the Central Intelligence Agency, the CIA, but there was to be no more active service overseas for Virginia. She spent the rest of her career in the USA, working behind a desk, planning and organising CIA activities around the world.

In 1950 Virginia and Paul were married, and when she was forced to retire from the CIA on age grounds in 1966 they settled on a farm in Maryland. From then, her days were spent peacefully reading, gardening, making cheese and looking after their dogs. Virginia Hall Golliot died on 12 July 1982, aged 76. Paul Golliot died five years later.

Virginia in later life

The British Government never gave up hope of formally awarding the wartime MBE that had been bestowed on Virginia. Finally, in 2006, they managed to locate her only surviving relative, her niece Lorna Catling. She was invited to a ceremony in Washington, attended by the British and French ambassadors. There, on 12 December, Miss Catling accepted the award, signed by King George VI, on Virginia's behalf.

the MBE

There is little doubt that Virginia Hall, and many spies like her, played a huge part in the Allies' ultimate victory in World War II. Without their daring deeds, British and American generals would not have had the top-secret information needed to form their battle plans. The spies' bravery not only saved soldiers' lives, but also helped to shorten the war, preventing further hardships and suffering for millions of civilians. Their war was spent in constant fear, waiting every minute for a knock at the door, or expecting someone to stop them as they walked on the street.

The risks for a spy were great – almost certain death if they were captured. The rewards for a spy were few. Spies might spend the rest of their lives without anyone realising the role they had played in saving their country from disaster.

Virginia Hall's passport, 1928

Spying in the 21st century

As the race to develop nuclear weapons gathered pace in the 1950s and 1960s, the role of the spy became even more vital. These agents operated in the backstreets and offices of Moscow, Berlin, London and other major capitals. Each government fought to keep its own secrets safe while stealing those of its rivals.

Today, almost every country in the world has its own intelligence service, but most information is now gathered from computers and mobile phones. Sophisticated listening stations pick up phone conversations from all over the world; computers are hacked and texts and emails are monitored. Satellites and CCTV cameras watch from the skies and on the ground.

However, despite the use of modern technology, spies still operate in much the same way as Virginia Hall did during World War II. Experts suggest that there are now more spies than ever operating in our cities, gathering information as they wait and watch.

Glossary

Allied	Britain and other countries fighting on the same side in World Wars I and II
antibiotics	medicines that fight bacterial infections
ammunition	bullets and shells
bayonets	stabbing blades fixed to rifles
black market	the illegal selling of government-controlled goods
charismatic	great personal charm that often inspires leadership
collaborators	people who side with an invading army during a war
consular service	officials representing the rights of their citizens in a foreign country
consulate	the building in which consular duties are carried out
decorated	received medals for bravery
defy	openly refusing to obey someone

detonators	charges that set off explosives
discriminate	single out for unfair treatment
dissatisfaction	unhappiness with an organisation or person
embassy	the residence of officials who represent their country abroad
enlisted	became a member of a military organisation
evasion	the act of avoiding something or someone
gruelling	very tough and tiring
harassed	bothered aggressively
patriotic	supporting your own country above all others
prearranged	organised beforehand
rationing	fixed amounts of food and goods to ensure everyone receives a fair share during wartime
regulations	rules set by those in authority
sabotaged	destroyed deliberately
safe house	a house in a secret location, used for protection
sympathisers	supporters of a group or point of view

Index

Virginia Hall's career

1931:
Virginia Hall joins the
US Consular Service

1 September 1939:
Germany invades Poland.
Virginia joins the
ambulance service in Paris

|—————•—————|—————•—————|—————|—————|—————|—————|—
1931   1933

December 1933:
loses left leg below the
knee in a hunting accident

June 1940:
France surrenders.
Virginia escapes to
England, joins the SOE
and trains to become a spy

1943:
is posted to Spain, but returns
to London within a few months
and trains as a radio operator

May 1945:
after World War ends
in Europe, Virginia is
awarded the
Distinguished
Service Cross and
returns to the USA

August 1941:
goes to France,
posing as an
American journalist

November 1943:
is awarded the MBE by
King George VI

1939   1940   1941   1942   1943   1944   1945

November 1942:
escapes France via
Spain to London

March 1944:
returns to France disguised
as a French peasant

Ideas for reading

Written by Clare Dowdall BA(Ed), MA(Ed)
Lecturer and Primary Literacy Consultant

Learning objectives: understand underlying themes, causes and points of view; understand how writers use different structures to create coherence and impact; sustain engagement with longer texts using different techniques to make the text come alive; improvise using a range of drama strategies and conventions to explore themes such as hopes, fears, desires; use different narrative techniques to engage and entertain the reader

Curriculum links: Geography: Passport to the world; History: What can we learn about recent history from studying the life of a famous person?

Interest words: diplomatic, dissatisfaction, consular service, Embassy, tourniquet, rationing, Resistance, sympathisers, intercepted, Gestapo, collaborators

Resources: whiteboard

Getting started

This book can be read over two or more reading sessions.

- Look at the front cover and read the blurb together. Ask children what they know about spies and whether they can name any from real life or fiction, e.g. James Bond.

- Explain that this book is a biography. Discuss what a biography is, and what its features will be, e.g. it is written about a real person, in the past tense.

- Discuss what children know about World War II and how they think spies would have been useful. Collect their ideas on a whiteboard.

Reading and responding

- Ask children to read Chapter 1, about Virginia Hall's early life, noting what prepared her for the life of a spy. Take children's ideas and discuss them, helping them to make inferences, e.g. travelling abroad from an early age because her family were wealthy.